BEFORE THEY SILENCE ME...

Lost Thoughts

Nuance Publishing

Nuance Publishing

www.nuancepublishing.com

I dedicate this book to the relationships
that have inspired my testimony

Table of Contents

Bittersweet

As the sunlight broke through the window blinds
And invited itself to lie across her naked flesh
I found myself running my fingers across her spine
Taking the time to memorize every line and curve
And as she laid there sleeping silently
I lost myself in sweet visions of the night we just
spent together
I made love to her with a passion that was soul deep
No longer was I looking to get a quick fix
But instead took my time to find every spot inside
the depths of her fantasies
That she longed for someone to touch
With every thrust, I aimed to leave her soul
pleased
And every soft release of breath let me know she was
The covenant that my flesh made with hers
Went beyond this world's definition of satisfaction

And as she climaxed, tears fell from her beautiful
brown eyes
And I knew for once in my life I was in the favor
of Christ
For she was my perfect match
My exact equal
My Rib
The only thing is
While I was hers...she was his

The Playground

Torn
As if ripped from the womb
Missing precious pieces of text
in this manuscript of me
I am a soul seeking shelter in my childhood ideals
Of Love, Happiness, and a Carefree existence
Roaming free in the playground of ignorance
Swinging from the monkey bars of innocence
Sliding down tubes of adversity
Scraped and scarred
Wounds I'd carry to my adult years; but
Homemade remedies take away the pain,
so I am free to go and play
Band-aids hide the marks
Allowing my inner-child another day
to lay among the stars
You see, I don't make love to my thoughts anymore

I fuck the shit out of my dreams
Planting the seed to birth the monument
of the man I intend to be
But my dreams are exhausted
Swollen shut and pain stricken
Far too long have I fucked my intentions
Frequently shifting my attention towards seducing
the essence of her innocence
I am nothing more than the source of her heartbreak
They call me "MC"
Mr. Carefree by any other name
breaks her heart the same
Seller of sweet dreams and pain
The barrier I'm building for the next man
Another brother is building for me in the heart
of the woman I am to call "My Queen"
I'm blind to the trouble I'm causing he
As he is ignorant to the trouble he is setting
in place for me
Too many "Adams" hurting "Eves"
Guiding her to the center of the Garden
and feeding her Forbidden Fruit from the Tree
Not of "Good and Evil", but of "Deceit and Mistrust'
All because our inner-child couldn't decipher
between Love and Lust

Forging forward until we have our fill
of fucking frequently
I find myself maturing to the place where sex
is the variable in our equation
I'd rather play with you in this sandbox
and have serious talks about
Which show was better... Fresh Prince of Bel-Air
or Martin?
The best days are those filled with your presence
and sweet silence
As our hearts race, wild in The Playground

I am Revolution

I am violet
Equal parts blue and red
That have been plastered and propagated
To extinguish the existence of the positive black
male image
In exchange for the fictitious often misjudged
violent barbarian
Baggy pants wearing, slick slang swearing
Big dick boasting, street educated
Money motivated, athletically gifted
Responsibility dodger, physical embodiment of the
antonym of "Father"
But to go a little further
I am the footsteps of Revolution
I am the most dangerous man in the room
Not because I have nothing to lose, but because
I have it all and no fear of losing it

Wisdom of experience and not age
Passed down through my veins from the
Slain, beaten, lynched, and flogged
I am the product of chain gangs, water hoses,
and dogs
Sit-ins, boycotts, long walks, and mountain
top talks
From peaceful assembly to boastful outbursts
I sit comfortable in my glass house, because I
won't cast my stone first
I'll wait until you realize my glass house
is bound in Faith
And my fate is far greater than those numbers
of any statistic
Where my value was limited to cooking in the
kitchen or washing the dishes
I am your greatest fear
The remedy to the self-perpetuating motion that
Willy taught you
When he came and spoke on how to lynch us
So, continue to push us but much like the slaves
that required Willy's attention
Prepare yourself for a revolution that the history
books must mention
This isn't a Black Poem, it's a humanity speech

How can you value your race then discredit mine
when we all will be judged by the Most High?
Buried and covered with dirt devoured by bugs
The next generations will build new kingdoms
upon us
Why make it more difficult for me when your own
storms will come?
The difference between you and me
Is I have learned how to play in the rain
While you stress in the sun
Why are you restraining your son?
We are the vessels carrying the blessings you've
been waiting to come
The youth don't need your every protection
We simply need you to testify, then step aside
So we can rise above your failed attempts at
progression
Feed us failure so we may defecate success and
where we fail
A new step will be laid for future generations to
make strides in past situations
Can't move forward if the past holds the power
And the most powerful time is this urgent hour
Who would have thought I would have to beg to
aid in progress?

So, I beg of you to be a part of this revolution
And marvel at the minds your underestimation
hasn't polluted

She Is God

He longs to feel her voice resonate through his soul
Shake his spirit to the core, so he may know LIFE
Expose Him
Strip him naked in front of a crowd
Not to be ridiculed, but to be admired
Appreciated and regarded as art
He is the PERFECT MAN
Beautifully flawed
Masterfully broken
Her masterpiece
She has exhausted her energy carving this Man
Shaving off the layers of childish games
Molding the mind and spirit until the material
had matured
Burned away arrogance, doubt, and self-pity
Leaving behind pure vulnerability

Painted the heart so the spirit radiates through
the eyes holding so much pain
Placed Him on a pedestal of pride and passion
He is hers... Not simply because of the work
she put into him
But because he knows he would still be a mound
of clay if it had not been for her
Trust and imagination
Commitment and consistency
Faith and purpose
She is his Creator
She... is... God

The Things I Meant to Say
When We Were Arguing

Talk to me... after you talk to God... so what you
say is not you, but He speaking to me
In a manner soothing to my ear describing where
these small steps will lead
In a larger picture that in this moment our Mortal
eyes can't seem to see beyond
Look at me as if I am always something new
to gaze upon
Let the sight of me be the twinkle of peace
in your eyes
As if to say my face is the first you want to see
when your spirit leaves your flesh
Let me be your vision of relief
Smell me first thing in the morning and fall
in love with my natural fragrance

19

That perfect blend of soap and my essence
that triggers memories
Of first dates, great conversations, and falling
asleep while the TV watches us
Close your eyes and glide your hands over the
contours of my frame
Place your fingertips over every imperfect inch
Long enough for me to know you will never forget
where I am ticklish
Kiss me and taste the passion that exudes
from my lips
That kiss that is so gentle, it is almost as if
our lips are barely touching
These lips where we emit the desires of our hearts
Through perfect reverence for He
who brought us to be... WE
For it is not truly me to whom you speak, feel,
hear, touch, or taste but He
For He is all things and our interaction
is simply the God in you
Falling in love with the God in me
Talk to me... after you hear from God...
So what will be between us is
What He would have us to be

Butterfly

I had a dream once
That I could hear the heartbeat of a butterfly
That had landed on the windowsill
Just outside of the room in which I was sitting
The butterfly's heartbeat was so fast, that it caused
her to move slightly with each pulse
And although subtle to my eye, it was clearly a
violent disruption to the butterfly
What could cause such a beautiful and elegant
creature so much distress?
Be so chaotic that she can't have peace even when
she's perfectly safe?
Where was she before coming to this place?
Who else had heard the butterfly pass by before
my eyes found her?
I cannot ignore her because her presence pulls my
attention like a moth to a flame

Maybe I am exactly who the butterfly needed to
hear her heartbeat
Because the moment I gave my attention to the
butterfly
My own thundering heart found peace
And in that moment I figured out my heartbeat
was the one I had heard
We should all be so lucky to hear a butterfly's
heartbeat in the middle of a storm

Oral Fix: A Sex Tale

Body shakes as he holds her
Spine tingles as he whispers
All the ways he loves her
But actions speak louder than words
And the verbs his grip emits from her voluptuous
curves
Only allows for faint whispers of nouns
Curves that leave his tongue tied
So words have to subside as he satisfies his oral fix
By licking and sucking on every orifice shaking her
foundation
As she lies on the bed exposed to the elements
Naked flesh releasing sweet aromas of Heaven's scent
He kneels in a position of complete submission
At this form that he knows is Heaven sent
No raunchy release can properly quench their long
restrained passions

She goes stiff as his tongues tip makes first contact
with her neck
Quick laps leave liquid tracks to her plump breast
Inhales and exhales cause deep heaves from her chest
And as she becomes accustomed to the motions of
his sucking
His hands find rest at the entrance of her moist lips
Sweet melodies laid into a symphony
Cause her sweet center to drip
He excites her sense of sight by sucking her
essence off his fingertips
Slowly he descends from breast to stomach
Stomach to belly button
Belly button to that ticklish
Oh so sensitive crease
Created by the thighs marriage to the waist
She braces as his breath paces back and forth
across her lips
His tongue reaches to separate her entrance
erasing memories of previous dissatisfaction
Air escapes her frame pushed out by ecstasy
He licks, he licks, he licks
She moves between each stroke
Letting each lick go deeper than the one that
preceded it
She isn't physically restrained

But her body is pinned down by the pressure
mounting beneath her surface
He moves from licking to sucking her legs wrap his
neck
Silence fills the room as her thighs squeeze tighter
about his head
She moans and groans as he becomes more
consistent in his oral dig
Hard work paying off as she reaches for objects not
present in the room
Sheets snatched off, back bent off of the bed
As the mounting pressure pushes against her
womb
He licks, he licks, he licks deeper into her crevice
She shudders and climaxes releasing all of that
mounted passion
His face drips... his oral fix quenched

Silhouette

Standing behind that sheer curtain, I see the
curves that shape my imagination
As you remove the binds of the linens that have
contained your rich mahogany for far too long
And let them fall soundlessly to the floor
Pulling at my senses with your senseless sensuality
Simply teasing my sight in the dim light emitted
from the candles you've lit
Your shadow bounces around the room playfully
Turning me on as if you've cloned yourself just for
me to experience other levels of your universe
One shadow falls on the bed; where you will
recover after we are finished
One on the wall; where I'm going to pin you
One on the ceiling; where your hands will be as
your thighs rest on my shoulders

Lost Thoughts

One on the floor; where my knees will meet carpet
as I taste your garden
One on the mirror; where you can see how my
backside clenches in climax
The last lying right across my waist; where my
nature awaits the first touch of your fingertips
The room is filled with your scent
I long to feel your breath heat up the spot behind
my left hear
Your teeth teasing my neck
While your hands trace my brands and tattoos
I am open to you
Vulnerable and willing to give you every ounce of
my emotion as we engage in our desires
The escape of that first breath after that first press
will be the first break in this deafening silence
Moan for me... as your body screams volumes of
pleasure from your warm opening
Press your skin to mine so tight I finally know
what having my rib back feels like
Our bodies move in synchronized motions to
music that only we can hear in the spaces between
breaths
Let mine be the name written on the walls...
Of your mind

For those moments when we are apart, I want you
to shift in your seat
As you reminisce on this night
You have me handcuffed to this chair
So I can't get to you from this side of the partition
I must rely on my imagination
And let my mind... make love... to your Silhouette

Black Woman

Tell me that you love me
But when you say it, I need you to say it in a way
that I forget all the others who
Said those same words before you
Make me believe it beyond this moment
Calculate exactly how close you need to be from
my ears as you speak those words
Say it so I know you have given it thought and it's
not just a reaction to avoid
An awkward interaction to my saying it first
Tell me you love me because you know I recognize
how amazing the small things about you are
Tell me because you know I lift you up void of
comparison to other women from my past
Tell me that you love me when I am low
For the genuineness in those words keep me
elevated in the midst of the storm

Tell me that you love me even when I am not in
sight
That is why your eyes don't fall upon another and
desire to give them more than a glance
I long to hear those words so I can tell you WHY I
love you...
I love you because in you I see my mother, sisters,
and daughter
I love you because I see strength, passion, and a
will to make me better by keeping me accountable
I love you because you are all that I desire to be; in
a vessel designed to create new life
I love you because without you, I am lacking a
counterpart
I love you because although others may apply for
the position, no one is better suited for the job
I love you because you challenge me daily
I love you because without you I am nothing more
than a man half-complete
I love you because you are more than a versatile
hairstyle
Legs attached to the prototype backside
Lips made to kiss
Skin coated in various flavors of mocha
Black woman you are the reason my success is note
worthy

God created me for you and you for me
Because we would otherwise be two lost ships
waiting to pass one another in the night
And although our PC society may disagree
There is no one better suited to Love you more
than me
So, please tell me you love me so this poem can be
more than words read by a few
Instead it shall serve as a testament to what a Black
man can be
When he matures enough to recognize
The BLACK WOMAN as Queen

The Right One

How long can you sit here and pretend that we are
just friends as if the years we've spent
Were just time fillers for another brotha to come
and take the love I've created for myself?
I'll be damned if I allow another man room
enough to be the source of your eye roll
Or the deliverer of your foot rub after a long day
away from home
And if I were better with the words, I'd write a
deeper love poem just to confess the mess
My life would be if you were not here;
and I were alone
Who people knew me as pales in comparison to
the man I am when my name is in your mouth
And if you are willing to give me a little bit
of a lifetime
I'd love to make a home out of this house

I will frustrate you and disappoint you, I will
apologize and make things right
I will accept being wrong even when I know I'm
right just to keep you a happy woman in our bed
at night
When we make love it'll be like every time is a
better time even though last time was the best time
And as we lay in stripes from the moonlight
coming through the blinds
I know who you are deep inside
You are the physical embodiment of a
conversation I had with God
20 plus years before this world recorded my life
When I asked him not to give me the woman of
my dreams
But to build me into the man I need to be for
The Woman created to be my Wife

Manhood

I am the prince of an empty kingdom
No one to rule with no one to rule over
Just a king to be with the weight of the world on
his shoulders
And my queen isn't a physical being
She is the culmination of sweet dreams and things
the imagination hasn't seen
How sweet the day will be when this "out of the
box" kind of love finds me
I am not a man shaken up by the idea of love
Nor the fear of failing at commitment
For that fear is just a commitment to failure
I've allowed the sweet nectar of flesh to derail my
focused mind
Exchanged her-
The Divine design that was uniquely mine
For a small waist with a thick behind

Falling into the tragic habit of those brothas who
brag about how they fuck like jack rabbits
With no intention on seeking greater ascension
into the depths of her
You see She was a rare beauty
First in her feminine bloodline to tell this man no
Wouldn't let me talk my way into her legs without
first finding home in her soul
She said I was not worthy of a gift so pure
And with that statement she somehow humbled
me
Unnatural reaction because under any other
circumstance my pride would have
Swelled up like a sting from a bumble bee
But that's the difference between love, lust, and
loyalty
The muse of my greatest poetry
Meant more to me than any good release
But when she left me
I felt like the city of Cleveland
Because who knew you could feel so cold with all
this talk about...Miami Heat
The heat that she provided could only be created
in the depths of a real woman
Free from immature flights of fancy about Prince

Charming's and Happily Ever After's
When she became a character in the book of me
My life became your favorite Zane chapters
Emotions exploding from the vivid imagery
And the shit that makes that bittersweet
Is as you continue your read you will come to find
that she is a million miles away from me
Not physically but emotionally Her inner woman
had reached the point that it was done growing
At least it was done growing with me
Because when she reached the deepest parts of me
she didn't find a man
In that space where a man should have stood was
simply a boy looking to get back on his path to
manhood
Unsure which way to go in order to be back in step
with her
7 Billion people on the planet and I've lost my way
home

If Life Were a Woman

Would you rush into her wonders head first or
take your time to mature through her layers
Become familiar with her from a distance
Before becoming intimate with her inner-workings
Learn to appreciate her subtle mood swings or be
broken by her wrath
Admire how she ages with grace or would you
critique her wrinkles
Take her out and control the entire conversation
or would you sit back and let her show you all and
more
Than you could ever ask for
Would you want her to be what you are used to
Or would you prefer she adds some spice to your
existence
Would you synch your steps with hers in a
beautiful dance

Or would you prefer to give her the stage as you sit
in the audience
Would you want another person to come along
and touch her
Or would you prefer to be the first and last kiss
she'll ever know
Could she come to you in despair and leave your
presence with a smile
Could you lay with her and memorize her lines
Make love to her and birth new days
Walk with her and create new pathways
If life was a woman... would she be dismissed
when you are done experiencing her passions
Or would she wake up next to you ready for new
adventures
Would you pray to have more of her
Would she pray to have more time with you
Sometimes we take life for granted
But much like a good woman
We learn too late just how boring we are... alone

If life were a woman... could you satisfy her?

The MOON

Would you notice the moon if it didn't move
around the Earth
If its pull didn't create waves
If it was just floating in the abyss
Would you notice it was missing if it didn't shift
your feelings?
As it shifted its phases
Waxing and waning
Entranced in this dance between the surface on
which you stand
And the life eternal that is waiting
Would you focus on the moons imperfections?
The surface that appears not to be able
to sustain life
Glowing and bright with a dark side

Craters left behind by years of impacts that have
chipped away at its gorgeous form
I could keep going with this poem, but it wouldn't
mean much
Because no one appreciates the moon
Until you say she's the life carrier endowed with a
womb
A woman who smiles all day just so you won't
know the depths of her pain
Tell her she is beautiful and mean what you are
saying because
Many have engaged her and none have left her
better or even the same
They have taken a glance at her finer parts and
stolen pieces of her away
She has been a conquest, but never a final
destination
Men that she welcomed into your pull
Staked their claim in their name then left prints
upon her essence she couldn't wipe away
Once she was conquered they returned
to where they came
Or moved on to another place where they believe
a better life could be sustained
Or greater conquest could be obtained

Would you notice the moon
if she was more beautiful?
If she came covered in hues of reds, greens, and blues
Draped in rouge or had an array of rings wrapped
about her being
Just to stand on the side of you
Can she go to bed and wipe away the various
shades and still be pleasing to the sight of you?
What happened to the days when she would wave
and the thought of being in her space excited you?
Maybe it's you, not her that has forgotten how
wonderful she is
She has adopted your thoughts and pressed them
upon herself for so long
She doesn't know who she is
That is why I count myself fortunate
That I can see beneath the rouge and the rings
Just how beautiful the moon is even when she has
her defenses up before me
She isn't just a destination
She is this man's foundation...
I don't have to see other moons or galaxies
Because I know my Moon is the perfect star
It doesn't matter if no one else recognizes my Moon
Because she knows that I can see

even beyond her scars
Just how perfect we are
Would you notice the Moon
I have locked inside my heart?

Before They Silence Me

Life is beautiful romance between differing
perspectives
Opportunity to grow presented in new-day second
chances
The romance between belonging and progression
Gets convoluted when the lens isn't standard
As children we are taught that the world
is ours to conquer
Then we grow up and realize our starting points
have been doctored
The rhetoric is all too familiar
And the things unsaid become the filler
For the awkward silence when race, religion, and
equality are the topic
The 'cultural stew' that those in peak position try
to serve you
Is filled with the ingredients of cultures that

they've consumed
These profit prophets only appreciate the beauty
of your racial background when they
can profit off it
Took people from their homes and forced labor
from their hands
We pay the oppressor to do a DNA test to tell us
what percentage of our genes came from what
land?
Tease us with the fact that we will have to journey
back in order to truly learn who we are
But this minimum wage can barely get me across
the state let alone across an ocean great
Packing the pockets of the system that has been
just as quick to dismiss us
Not to mention the complete dismissal of any
obligation of reparations
Neglecting historical contexts because it's easier to
teach alternative facts
Nation born from refugees escaping religious
persecution, to an exclusive Constitution
Where the female counterpart was dismissed and
minority rights were a delusion
Irony of the past repeating
We know what's right, but perception
is misleading

When you are advantaged you have the privilege
of not even seeing that the problems of millions
Could be fixed through your convincing
Our Fight with Your Voice
Your Power with our Resilience
We know the system wasn't created for us all
When do we fix the foundation of this building?
It started to crumble when the silent found their
voice
The laborers began to rise
When violence couldn't quiet the riots
Or comfort the cries
Of millions of people tired of feeding lifelong
famine with hearty historical lies
From the mouths of the elders
We scream "STILL I RISE"
From the mouth of revolution
We scream "WE GONE BE ALRIGHT"
I am the brain that Tupac sparked that will change
the world
Before They Silence Me... I will...
(To be continued)

Suicide's Surrender

With the last breaths of my life I shall be still
Cool, calm, and collected
Mind and spirit at peace as I release the final
palpitations of my chest
I will flat line... Alone
No hands to hold or eyes to stare into
No one to tell "I love you"
I will go alone

Leaving this world all that I had to give
There will be no need for me to make peace with
any human being
No need to waste my last breaths asking for
forgiveness
No confessions of sins between friends
No heart to heart with my "Rib born" counterpart
Because they will not be there

Lost Thoughts

The pain a smile hides are far beyond those I'd
bring to light

And if you could see into my life, you would know
why my mother named me Sky
I was born into a world not ready to know me and
Like an over eager teenage boy I tried to force
myself upon her
Now she lies stained in garments of fear and
scarlet
Wrapped in despair and disbelief that I would take
advantage of her in this lifetime
But when I ask her what other options I had?
All the world could say was reply...

You were born a step behind because you are dark
as night,
Your blood is stained by the pre-marital exchange
of fluids between a teenager and tourist
Who could not see the beauty of your mother's
landscape
You are a misfit whose life has been enumerated
in statistics
I knew you were not worthy of the best of me
that's why I've given you all of my bullshit

What kind of world would look at me and say
this?
I was taught I was an African warrior ripped
straight from the history pages
A single entity in the bloodline of the first human
beings spoken into time
From the mouth of the Most High
Yet you tell me you only see a man not worthy
enough to edify
So on this day, I shall commit suicide
Leaving behind the love of my life and my child
I could never explain the pain hidden behind my
smile
And to do so is simply not worthwhile

This is my letter of peace
The demons my mistakes have created have left
me no room to release
The pulpit in which I sit on Sunday morn has left
me condemned
And in a circle of friends I see only strange faces
among familiar men
Where does one go when Home is an unfamiliar
place even when it's where your heart is?
God, please forgive me for I have sinned

Taken the gifts you've given and have completely
wasted my talents
My poetry has served me in releasing my limited
human understanding of a universe
Far greater than this 8–5 life I wake up to every
A.M.
I'd much rather return to the days of sandboxes
and monkey bar playing
When life's most serious question was "Why are
there no black super sayians?"
But since my DeLorean can't take me back to the
hay-day
I'd much rather make way for the next
Generation of condemned children who'll be
forced to live in the hell
That our mistakes have made

A poet's goodbye is a real loss... Lost words... lost
memories... Lost thoughts...
My pen is my knife and with this pen I shall slice
from my wrist straight up to my shoulder
Leaking all over my room in painful silence as I
realize in death I will miss the sweet sounds of quiet
Sounds of sarcastic remarks from my best friend
who was soon to be my best man

The touch of my daughter's small hands
Or the kiss of my "Dot" that made my heart stop
when I was too young and dumb to know that
In that Kiss I was experiencing what real love was

Too much life to live, so from wrist to page, I move
this pen...
I HAVE TOO MUCH LIFE TO LIVE
But when God calls me home, I will have given all
I was born to give
So I surrender